Keeping Fit

by Emily K. Green

BLASTOFF!
2
READERS

BELLWETHER MEDIA • MINNEAPOLIS, MN

Note to Librarians, Teachers, and Parents:

Blastoff! Readers are carefully developed by literacy experts and combine standards-based content with developmentally appropriate text.

Level 1 provides the most support through repetition of high-frequency words, light text, predictable sentence patterns, and strong visual support.

Level 2 offers early readers a bit more challenge through varied simple sentences, increased text load, and less repetition of high-frequency words.

Level 3 advances early-fluent readers toward fluency through increased text and concept load, less reliance on visuals, longer sentences, and more literary language.

Whichever book is right for your reader, Blastoff! Readers are the perfect books to build confidence and encourage a love of reading that will last a lifetime!

This edition first published in 2007 by Bellwether Media.

No part of this publication may be reproduced in whole or in part without written permission of the publisher. For information regarding permission, write to Bellwether Media Inc., Attention: Permissions Department, Post Office Box 1C, Minnetonka, MN 55345-9998.

Library of Congress Cataloging-in-Publication Data
Green, Emily K., 1966–
  Keeping fit / by Emily K. Green.
    p. cm. — (Blastoff! readers) (New food guide pyramid)
Summary: "A basic introduction to the health benefits of keeping fit. Intended for kindergarten through third grade students."
  Includes bibliographical references and index.
  ISBN-10: 1-60014-006-8 (hardcover : alk. paper)
  ISBN-13: 978-1-60014-006-8 (hardcover : alk. paper)
  1. Physical fitness—Juvenile literature. 2. Exercise—Juvenile literature. I. Title. II. Series.
  RA781.G7977 2007
  613.7'1—dc22
                                                    2006000410

Text copyright © 2007 by Bellwether Media.
Printed in the United States of America.

Table of Contents

Kids need good food and **exercise** to be healthy.

The Food Guide Pyramid

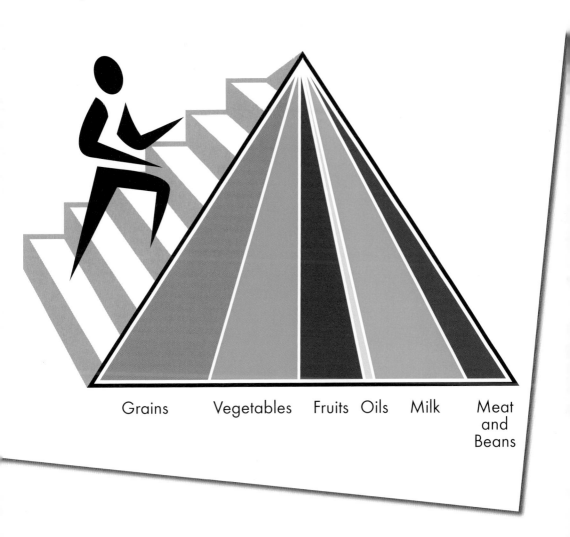

Grains Vegetables Fruits Oils Milk Meat and Beans

Exercise is part of the **food guide pyramid.**

Exercise can make your **muscles** stronger.

Riding a bike is good exercise. It helps you build strong muscles.

Exercise makes your heart strong and healthy.

Anna swims. Her heart is
strong and healthy.

Exercise can help you keep a healthy **weight**.

Max and Pete play
basketball. They keep a
healthy weight.

Exercise can help you
make friends.

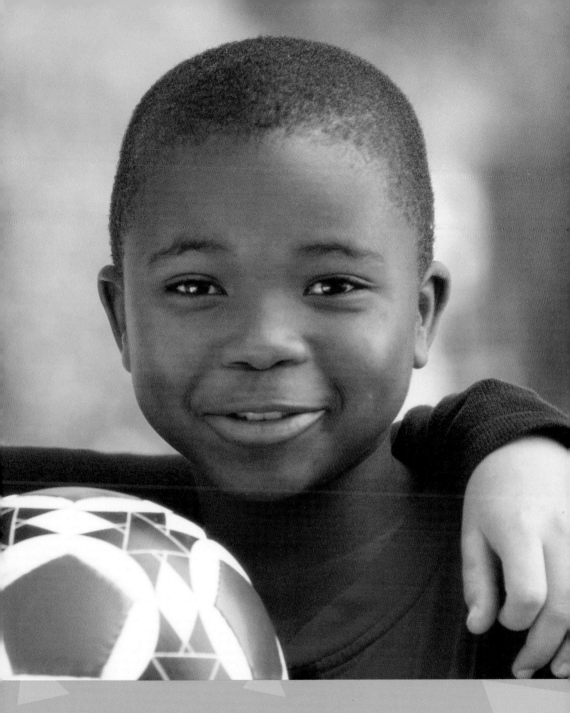

James and Joe play soccer together. They are good friends.

Exercise can help you feel calm and happy.

Pam plays softball. She
feels calm and happy
after the game.

Racing is an exciting way to exercise.

Jenny races her way to a healthier body.

Try spending time with your
family when you exercise.

Skating together helps
everyone in this family
stay healthy.

You should exercise for an hour every day.

Exercise is fun.
So get moving!

Glossary

exercise—to put effort into moving your body to stay fit and stay healthy

food guide pyramid—a chart showing the kinds and amounts of foods you should eat each day

muscles—parts of your body that help you move

weight—how much something weighs

To Learn More

AT THE LIBRARY
de Brunhoff, Laurent. *Babar's Yoga for Elephants.*
New York: Harry N Abrams, 2002.

Rockwell, Lizzy. *The Busy Body Book: A Kid's Guide
to Fitness.* New York: Crown, 2004.

Thomas, Pat and Lesley Harker. *My Amazing Body:
A First Look at Health and Fitness.* New York:
Barrons, 2002.

ON THE WEB

Learning more about keeping
fit is as easy as 1, 2, 3.

1. Go to www.factsurfer.com

2. Enter "keeping fit" into the search box.

3. Click the "Surf" button and you will see a list of
   related web sites.

With factsurfer.com, finding more information is just a
click away.

Index

The photographs in this book are reproduced through the courtesy of: Alistair Berg/ Getty Images, front cover; Stephanie Rau/Getty Images, p. 4; Premium Stock/Getty Images, pp. 6-7; Peter Cade/ Getty Images, pp. 8-9; Ty Allison/Getty Images, pp. 10-11; Arthur Tilley/Getty Images, pp. 12-13; Mary Lane, pp. 14-15; Jim Cummins/Getty Images, pp. 16-17; Lori Adamski Peek/Getty Images, pp. 18-19; Tammy McAllister, p. 20; Jaimie Duplass, p. 21.